HOW TO GET OVER
AN ADDICTION

Ad·dic·tion:

"a compulsive, chronic, physiological or psychological need for a habit-forming substance, behavior, or activity."

howtolifegood

To get access to the video accompanying this PDF (if you haven't already done so), please use the coupon code below. Simply go to www.howtolifegood.com, choose this topic, and type in the following coupon code.

R76SFL9

We all have a propensity for being addicts. As humans, we are pattern-loving creatures. We implement patterns in our lives to maximize simplicity and limit the amount of thinking we are required to do. It's biologically advantageous. Living with patterns allows us to focus our emotional and intellectual energy on the novel, and possibly threatening, aspects of our lives.

In addition, at a base level humans seek to maximize comfort and minimize pain. We want to increase our good feelings and experiences, and limit the difficult ones. There's nothing wrong with this dynamic. It's perfectly reasonable we would want to have a positive life and lifestyle. However, when we experience pain—either in the present or the past—we can be drawn to wanting to apply comfort. Comfort can be a healthy expression (exercise, therapy, good conversations, etc.). However, as with all things they can be done to the extreme.

At the negative end of the spectrum are our addictions. Addictions are our attempts to minimize pain and maximize pleasure. Unfortunately, addictions do so in a destructive way. Addictions cause us to numb our emotional pain and give us short-term pleasure at the expense of long-term rewards. The "pay-off" of our addictions is very real. If there wasn't a payoff to addictions we could easily discard them as a limiting pattern that is unhealthy for us.

Further complicating the issue is just how many different addictions are possible. Here are just a few of the major categories: intimacy disorders, sex, workaholism, substance abuse, TV or Video game over-use, over-eating, under-eating, etc.

If you are reading this booklet, you are probably aware of a few addictions you are currently abusing, or some that have been present in your past. It's rare for someone to not have any addictive behavior or patterns. That doesn't mean that we shouldn't endeavor to free ourselves from these negative patterns.

The more we can address our addictions, and overcome their negative influences, the happier and more connected we will live. Having an addiction is a form of imprisonment. It may not be as tangible as the bars and concrete of a jail-cell, but it can be just as suffocating. In essence, we feel out of control of ourselves, and under the control of the addiction.

As we will explain later in this booklet, addictions are often rooted in positive patterns. As explained above, addictions are our attempts to avoid pain and maximize comfort. So, take the extreme example of a young child who is molested. During their molestation they learned to "escape" into fantasy and shut down any sexual engagement. You wouldn't blame that child/person when they escape to fantasy when they are an adult. It was a protective response to a traumatic experience, and it became hard-wired when the person grew up.

Another example is an over-eater. When the person was younger, they may have had a traumatic (or neglectful) environment. As an attempt to manage and minimize their pain, they learned to comfort eat. It became a pattern every time something difficult or unexpected came up they went to their default: food. As a child who was out of control of their environment and parents, it is reasonable that a child would choose to comfort themselves through something as accessible as food. As an adult, it can be a painful hold-over causing more negative effects than positive.

Yet another example is a child who grows up with parents who constantly fight. The child learns to "check out" and minimize their expressed needs (because they don't want to add more stress to the household). They stuff their emotions, and learn to pacify themselves through TV and video games. When they become older, their methods evolve as they discover alcohol, tobacco, and drugs. They adapted their "checking out" into whatever was available.

The point being, getting over an addiction can feel complicated. It can be overwhelming, and it can feel extremely vulnerable to face those aspects of our lives. When we address our addictions, in reality, we are confronting our biggest fears and releasing long-harbored emotions. The addiction is simply the symptom of something underlying...that has likely been a part of your make-up for an extremely long time.

Don't be surprised if you feel many emotions you haven't felt for a long time. These emotions will likely surface at a much younger age, which can make us feel even more vulnerable. It's also why our minds don't seem to "work right" when we are in the middle of releasing harbored emotions.

The good news is that addictions are caps to our lives. They keep our emotions numb, our intimacy limited, and passion and purposes dormant. When we remove addictions from our lives, we will become sober to our clarity, power, and the enjoyment of life.

DISCLAIMER:
Facing addictions requires asking ourselves painful questions. This booklet will unquestionably challenge you, but will also guide you into a lifestyle you have long-desired.

This booklet is broken into 5 major sections:

1. The Cost

2. The Benefit

3. The Cluster

4. The Process

5. Conclusion - Your True Identity

SECTION 1:
THE COST

Being honest about our addiction is difficult. What's even more difficult is the many costs of having an addiction. Most of the time we minimize the costs because it is too psychologically difficult to face them all at once.

The costs are sometimes conspicuous, and other times are deeply hidden. The costs include hurting ourselves, others, financial pains, loss of productive work, decreased creativity, lack of clarity, limited intimacy with those we love, etc. The list of costs could be dozens long, but for our purposes, we'll focus on the most pronounced.

1 *What are addictions you either have or have had in your life:*

- [ ] Pornography
- [ ] Sex Addict
- [ ] Relationship Addiction
- [ ] Drug Abuse
- [ ] Affairs
- [ ] Workaholism
- [ ] Self Improvement
- [ ] Shame
- [ ] Video Games

- [ ] TV or Digital Media
- [ ] Rage
- [ ] Alcohol
- [ ] Tobacco
- [ ] Shopaholism
- [ ] Kleptomania
- [ ] Over-Exercising
- [ ] Other _____

2 *How long have you struggled with your addiction(s)?*

_____

_____

_____

_____

3 *Have you attempted to stop in the past?*

- [ ] Yes
- [ ] No

4 *If so, how long were you sober from your addiction?*

_____

5 *What methods have you used in the past to get over your addiction?*

- [ ] Accountability Partners
- [ ] Therapy
- [ ] Hypnotism
- [ ] Mentorship
- [ ] White-knuckling
- [ ] Cold Turkey Quitting
- [ ] Support Groups

- [ ] Read Books
- [ ] Watched Videos
- [ ] Confessing
- [ ] Apps or Website Support
- [ ] Other _____
- [ ] Other _____

6 *Were any of the aforementioned attempts successful? Why or why not?*

_____

_____

_____

_____

_____

7 *How has your addiction cost you personally?*

_____

_____

_____

_____

_____

8 *How has your addiction impacted your work?*

_____

_____

_____

_____

_____

9 *How has your addiction impacted your romantic relationships?*

_____

_____

_____

_____

10 *How has your addiction impacted your other relationships (be as specific as possible)?*

_____

_____

_____

_____

11 *If you had to guess the total amount you have spent on your addiction—and the amount it has cost you financially in indirect ways—how much would you estimate? Include the costs of habit, career inhibition expenses, length of addiction, etc.*

_____

_____

_____

_____

12 *If you could rewind to the beginning of your addiction, and imagine that you had never started, how would you believe your life would have turned out differently?*

_____

_____

_____

_____

_____

_____

_____

_____

13 What are the potential risks of your behavior that haven't yet come to fruition (for example, cancer, getting caught by spouse and divorced, losing job, resentful children, etc.)?

_____

_____

_____

_____

_____

_____

14 How would your spouse or significant other feel if they knew the extent of the problem? Or how would you imagine they would feel if you were married?

_____

_____

_____

_____

_____

_____

_____

15 How would your family feel if they knew the extent of the addiction?

_____

_____

_____

_____

16 Are you hiding your addiction from anyone? Or are you selectively sharing information about your addiction? Why do you believe you do this?

_____

_____

_____

_____

17 *Fast forward your life 5 years, and imagine you are still acting out in your addiction. What do you visualize your life would look and feel like?*

_____

_____

_____

_____

18 *How motivated are you to get out of your addiction?*

Not at All   Medium Interested   Desperate for Change

1   *2*   *3*   *4*   *5*   *6*   *7*   *8*   *9*   *10*

19 *What do you think would increase your motivation for quitting your addiction?*

_____

_____

Exercise:

Write a letter to your addiction. In the letter, personify your addiction as if you were talking to someone right in front of you. Be as honest as you can, and tell your addiction how it has impacted your life. Explain the costs you have borne and the difficulties it has brought into your life. Let yourself feel the positives or negatives of being in "relationship" with your addiction.

SECTION 2:
THE BENEFITS

THERE ARE TWO SIDES TO THE BENEFITS OF ADDICTIONS.

1 **The first side is the benefit (pay-off) of the addiction.**

It is essentially the reason we are in the addiction in the first place, and the pay-off that keeps us in the pattern.

2 **The second type of benefits occurs when the addiction is ceased.**

These benefits are what happens when an addiction is no longer an active part of the person's life. These include financial improvements, career clarity, romantic relationship improvements, etc. Some of these can be quantified: *I make more money.* Others are intangible: *I just feel so much better!*

In this section, we're going to explore the benefits that have kept you in the addiction <u>and</u> the benefits of getting out of it.

"Benefits" of the Addiction

1 *When did you first start your addiction? (Were you exposed to pornography as a kid? Start smoking in college? Got positive feedback for being an over-performer in sports? Etc.)*

_____

_____

_____

_____

2 *What was the motivation for you to first engage with the activity?*

_____

_____

_____

_____

3 *What were your initial feelings around the activity?*

_____

_____

_____

_____

4 *When did you realize that your habit could be potentially?*

_____

_____

_____

_____

5 *What were/are the "benefits" of your addiction?*

- ☐ Fun
- ☐ Relaxes Me
- ☐ Blunts Emotions
- ☐ Feel Connected
- ☐ Feel Valued
- ☐ Exciting
- ☐ Need to Check Out

- ☐ Feel Alive
- ☐ Feel Connected
- ☐ Feel Attractive
- ☐ Other: _____
- ☐ Other: _____
- ☐ Other: _____
- ☐ Other: _____

6 *What would be the benefits of quitting (or drastically minimizing) your addiction?*

- ☐ Feel More Connected
- ☐ Improved Work
- ☐ More Creativity
- ☐ Feel Proud (less shame)
- ☐ Less Stress
- ☐ Don't Have to Hide
- ☐ Can Connect with Family

- ☐ More Money
- ☐ More Energy
- ☐ More Confidence
- ☐ Other: _____
- ☐ Other: _____
- ☐ Other: _____
- ☐ Other: _____

7 *What would be the benefits of my quitting to my spouse or significant other (or future significant other)?*

_____

_____

_____

_____

8 *What would be the benefit to my family of my quitting?*

_____

_____

_____

_____

9 *How would you feel about yourself if you were able to quit and maintain sobriety?*

_____

_____

_____

_____

10 *What are the aspects of your personality you believe have been inhibited by your addiction (confidence, warmth, intelligence, personability, etc.)?*

_____

_____

_____

_____

11 *If you were "counseling" someone in your position with an addiction, what advice would you give them?*

_____

_____

_____

_____

12 *Does that advice apply to you? Why or why not?*

_____

_____

_____

_____

Exercise:

Use your answers from this section to create two columns. In column 1, write down all of the "benefits" of your addiction. Be HONEST! It's okay to admit that some of these benefits feel good or have legitimate value in our lives. Next to each benefit, write a number between 1 and 10. 1 means that the benefit is relatively unimportant or undesirable. A level 10 would mean that it is exceptionally important and valuable to you.

In another column, write all of the benefits of living without your addiction. Using the same scale (1 to 10) write down the value of the benefits of living sans-addiction.

After you complete both of your columns and valuations, add up the addiction benefit column and put the number at the bottom. Likewise, add up the benefits for living addiction-free and put the number at the bottom. Use your answers to determine the value of the "benefits" of your addiction.

When you finish, it should look like an expanded version of this list below:

Pornography

Addiction YES		Addiction NO	
See Naked Girls	7	Feel Confident	9
Stress Reliever	6	Feel Clean	8
Numb Emotions	4	Close to Wife	9
Feels Exciting	7	No Shame	10
	24		36

SECTION 3:
THE CLUSTER

1 What do you consider your primary addiction (the one most prominent and destructive in your life)?

_____

_____

2 What are your secondary addictions? These addictions may not even be currently utilized in your life, but are potentially lurking in the background?

1. _____

2. _____

3. _____

4. _____

3 Do you have multiple addictions currently at play in your life? What are they?

_____

_____

_____

_____

4 Have you addiction-switched in your life before? What happened?

_____

_____

_____

_____

5 If you quit your primary addiction, do you believe you could also refrain from your secondary addictions? Why or why not?

_____

_____

_____

_____

6 Who are my friends that know about my addiction? Are they enabling me?

_____

_____

_____

_____

7 *What changes would you need to make in your community to confidently become sober?*

_____

_____

_____

_____

8 *Who are friends/community members who would be a positive support in a "sobriety journey"?*

_____

_____

_____

_____

Exercise:

Visualize yourself without your addictions. Fast-forward your life a year or two, and imagine letting go of one addiction after another. Let yourself explore what it feels like to not be wrestling with any addictions.

Go into different scenarios in your life (family time, work, rest) and let yourself feel your new life-posture. It's okay if some of the emotions are not positive! It is likely you will feel scared, overwhelmed, or revealed in that place. Instead of responding to those emotions reflexively, allow yourself to accept them as normal parts of growing and your humanity. It's okay to not be okay! Allow yourself to become comfortable in your discomfort.

SECTION 4:
THE PROCESS

If you've made it this far, congratulations! The initial few sections were intended to "til the soil" in your psychology. They weren't designed to be the process to lead you out of your addiction, but simply help you gain clarity and objectivity about it. Ironically, many of us avoid directly facing our addictions for fear of being overwhelmed only to find that it provides clarity and freedom.

The process has many elements for lasting sobriety. In this section, we are going to address some of the most important components. For example, having a supportive community, understanding the cause of the addiction, making a plan, finding healthy replacements, etc.

To simplify the process, we're going to explore what an addiction is (in laymen's terms) and why it is so difficult to treat.

Addictions are simply a way to inhibit our pain. The pain may be occurring in the present or rooted in the past; regardless, addictions are our attempts to escape it. Many studies have shown that pursuing pleasure is highly motivating, but avoiding pain is even more motivating. In essence, our addictions are our ways to pacify our emotions and comfort ourselves.

In my practice, I see a lot of veterans. And almost to a man (or woman), they would rather run at bullets than feel their harbored pain. It can be terrifying! It is scary because when we experienced most of these difficult situations we didn't have comfort or connection (otherwise, we would have processed them out). Feeling these emotions can make us feel isolated and exposed.

In our present day lives, we likely have a much more developed set of tools to address our emotions more compassionately. We can have grace for our more dramatic emotions, we can invite people into them, or we can expose them to a loving God. The important part, however, is that we feel "connected" when we are doing it. If we are just trying to feel emotions for the sole intention of releasing them, we are still compartmentalized. We are trying to "fix" ourselves, instead of attempting to be compassionate and connected to ourselves.

The good news is our emotions are often not nearly as overwhelming as they first appear. I have had numerous situations, with myself and my clients, where a terrifying emotion passed in ten minutes of my confronting it. It's not a guarantee, but it happens.

The key is to accept our emotions. When you start to have large emotions surface, just say to yourself, "this is okay, this is healthy, and it's very human for me to have emotions about what has happened." When you become okay with not feeling "emotionally okay" you'll find a sense of peace...and you'll process out your emotions with much more clarity and grace. By being compassionate with yourself, you'll also be connecting with your emotions and likely inviting others (or God) into experiencing your emotions with you.

Trying to feel your emotions without connection or compassion is the opposite; it is tormenting! We feel tormenting emotions when we feel isolated and not compassionate with them. This "disconnected" emotional processing is what causes us to avoid emotions in the first place.

Imagine a really kind, present father. When his son is hurt by a bully at school the father is present, compassionate, and allows his son to feel angry and sad. The son will likely release these powerful emotions. Now, let's imagine a scenario with an absent father. The same boy had the same experience, but there was no one to create a safe and connected environment for his feelings. Feeling his emotions in an isolated

isolated way is overwhelming and not comforting. This same example parallels our being connected and compassionate with ourselves.

Secondly, addictions are often our ways of maintaining a familiar level of stress. When we are younger, we are exposed to a relatively consistent level of stress. This familiar stress level feels normal, and comfortable (even when extremely dramatic, traumatic, or painful). As we grow older, we have internalized this stress level, and we will seek to maintain it.

As an example, let's say that your childhood was extremely difficult due to neglect and consistent fighting in the house. When you grow older, you may feel uncomfortable with a peaceful environment or relationship. Your response, subconsciously, may be to recreate your "normal" stress levels by introducing an addiction: porn, fighting, escapism, etc.

Another example is the workaholic father. If your father wasn't present in the home, it models a template that you will likely recreate in your adulthood. In response, you may either become a workaholic yourself, marry one, or choose a substance that gives the same "non-present" feel of workaholism.

One more insidious aspect of addictions is their short-term reward system. An addiction is quick and easy to engage in. Want to smoke; you can smoke a cigarette almost instantaneously. Stressed out; you can start playing games on your phone in a matter of seconds. In other words, the amount of time between a craving and the fulfillment of the craving is very short.

On the other hand, abstinence from an addiction has a longer-term reward system. You may not see the "rewards" for days, weeks, or even months. It takes time to develop new habits, normalize a sober existence, etc.

Take over-eating as an example. You can grab an ice cream from the store in 10 minutes. But it can take months of diligence to start to lose enough weight to recognize the pay-off. The beautiful, and redeeming part, is that abstaining from an addiction has much, MUCH larger rewards. And often, these are the most foundationally satisfying rewards; healthier relationships, work enjoyment, clarity in life, feeling healthier, more money, etc. But, in order to end our instant pay-off relationship with our addictions we have to form new, stronger relationships with the longer-term payoff of healthy behaviors.

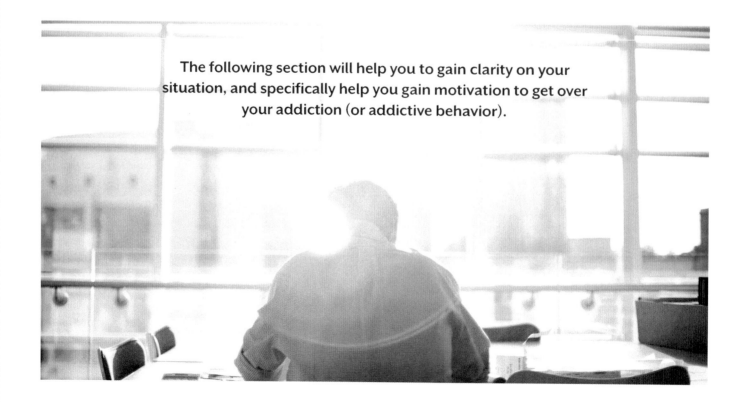

The following section will help you to gain clarity on your situation, and specifically help you gain motivation to get over your addiction (or addictive behavior).

1   *What is the no. 1 reason you want to get free of your addiction?*

_____

_____

_____

_____

2   *What are some of your other reasons for getting free of your addiction?*

        a.   _____

        b.   _____

        c.   _____

        d.   _____

        e.   _____

        f.   _____

        g.   _____

        h.   _____

        i.   _____

        j.   _____

3   *Why do you believe you've been unsuccessful in the past?*

_____

_____

_____

_____

4   *Why do you believe you've been unsuccessful in the past?*

_____

_____

_____

_____

5 *Write out how your life will play out if you don't discontinue your addiction?*

_____

_____

_____

_____

_____

_____

_____

_____

6 *Write out how your life will play out if you discontinue your addiction?*

_____

_____

_____

_____

_____

_____

_____

_____

7 *What is your initial plan for getting free of your addiction(s)? For example, go cold turkey, incrementally reduce the amount of acting out, etc.*

_____

_____

_____

_____

8 *Who are supportive people you can be 100% transparent with about your process?*

_____

_____

_____

_____

9 How will you marshall their support or oversight?

_____

_____

_____

_____

10 What emotions come up when you think of implementing an end to your addiction (overwhelmed, scared, hopeless, powerless, angry, etc.)?

_____

_____

_____

11 How are you going to healthily deal with emotions that surface (bring someone else in, journal, go to support group, etc.)?

_____

_____

_____

12 To become sober, you'll need alternative activities for when you get triggered or have vulnerable free time. Tick options you might employ instead of acting out. And then, write ten of your own options.

☐ Play with my kids   ☐ Go to a movie
☐ Talk to spouse   ☐ Read a book
☐ Exercise   ☐ Clean my room/closet
☐ Go for a walk   ☐ Paint a room
☐ Journal   ☐ Do a hobby I enjoy

Additional Alternative Activities:

1. _____   6. _____

2. _____   7. _____

3. _____   8. _____

4. _____   9. _____

5. _____   10. _____

13 *Why <u>do you</u> believe it is important to stop this negative behavior?*

_____

_____

_____

_____

14 *What is your plan for when you "slip up"? Note: slip ups are a part of becoming abstinent. It's important we know how to re-engage with our sobriety program quickly after breaching abstinence.*

_____

_____

_____

_____

15 *What is something you can do on a daily basis to remind yourself of why you are fighting for sobriety? Ex. Write 5 main reasons to get sober, write 5 identity statements about who you truly are, do a 10 minute meditation daily, etc.*

_____

_____

_____

_____

16 *What is your initial goal for sobriety (1 day, 1 week, 1 month, etc.)? What is a way you can track your progress (calendar, etc.)?*

_____

_____

_____

_____

17 *What rewards do you want to put in place for various milestones? For example, treat yourself to a journal, movie, etc. when you hit one week.*

_____

_____

_____

_____

18 *What is your level of confidence in your sobriety (1 being not at all hopeful and 10 being supremely confident).*

1   2   3   4   5   6   7   8   9   10

19 *What would improve your degree of confidence if you implemented it into your plan?*

_____

_____

_____

_____

20 *What is one disempowering statement of belief you need to confront in order to be successful (for example, I don't think I can do this, I'm scared, I've tried so many times before this isn't going to work either)?*

_____

_____

_____

_____

21 *What is a positive response to your disempowering "statement of belief" above?*

_____

_____

_____

_____

22 *How will you feel after the following intervals of time sober? Be as descriptive, visual, and emotional as possible.*

1 Day: _____

_____

1 Week: _____

_____

1 Month: _____

_____

1 Year: _____

_____

5 Years: _____

_____

10 Years: _____

_____

Quick Note:

We often approach sobriety as if it is a huge monster we are fighting. This is a component of addiction. The deception that sobriety is difficult, impossible, hopeless keeps us trapped in our addiction. It's time to view addiction as something that is easy, exciting, motivating, and inspiring.

23 *Responding to the "quick note" above, what are the feelings you WANT to feel about the sobering process?*

_____

_____

_____

_____

23 *What are your reservations about becoming sober?*

_____

_____

_____

_____

24 *How would you address those reservations with someone else?*

_____

_____

_____

_____

25 *What do you need in place for your successful sobering (ex. Community, to not go to bars, not to drink alone, etc.)?*

_____

_____

_____

_____

26 *Write an empowering statement about your transition to sober living (Ex. I am going to cease drinking...because I want to be a good father and husband).*

I am going to: _____

_____

_____

Because: _____

_____

_____

_____

Exercise:

Write a letter to yourself. In the letter, apologize to yourself. Explain all of the ways that your addiction has robbed from you, and those you love. Be as specific and thorough as possible. This is not an opportunity for you to exploit your shame, but instead to empower you to take honest responsibility for the costs of your addiction.

SECTION 5: CONCLUSION - YOUR TRUE IDENTITY

Sobriety has four basic levels to address.

1
Physical Addiction

2
Emotional Addiction

3
Relational Addiction

AND

4
Identity

Identity is "the characteristics determining who...a person is." Identity is our self-understanding. We can have false understandings of our identity, and true ones. The false understandings of our identity come from difficult circumstances or relationships, modeling, trauma, etc. We absorb "un-truths" about our identities based on our experiences.

For example, if our mom or dad is not present in our lives, we might subconsciously believe that we are unworthy of love. Our false identity will cause us to seek future experiences that validate our unworthiness. We may find mates that are emotionally unavailable, or allow others to exploit us sexually because we don't believe we are worthy of love or value.

All of us have impurities in our identities. They cause us to make mistakes, numb out, and reenact painful aspects of our history. Inevitably, we will be uncovering aspects of our false identity, and hopefully, uncovering our authentic identities.

Our authentic identities are God-designed. They are good. Positive. Deep feeling. Worthy of respect and positive treatment. They are powerful, substantive, and full of life, joy, and enthusiasm. The value of our authentic identities CANNOT be overstated.

It is our understanding of our true identities that allow us to treat ourselves in positive ways. As an example, we may not want to "mistreat" ourselves through an addiction. An addiction would be in contrast to our sense of self. It would be abrasive to our self-value, self-respect, and the life we understand we are meant to live. In other words, addictions have no place in the lives of someone who deeply knows and honors their identity.

A good metaphor, as first shared by Zig Ziglar, was that of a race horse. A race horse is valuable. It is treated exceptionally well by staff, trainers, owners, and even by riders. A race horse is given exceptional food, high quality water, and a healthy schedule of exercise. Put simply, if a race horse is treated so well because it's value is recognized, how much more are we to recognize our value and treat ourselves accordingly?

In this final section of his book, you will be asked about your identity and be given direction on clarifying your identity and value.

1 *How do you view yourself?*

_____

_____

_____

2 *What are positive qualities you possess?*

_____

_____

_____

3 *What are negative qualities you possess?*

_____

_____

_____

4 *Do you believe these negative qualities are authentic to your God-given design? Why or why not?*

_____

_____

_____

5 *How would you describe your FALSE identity? (Ex. Sarah is an alcoholic who is always stressed out...)*

_____

_____

_____

6 *Do you believe you are worthy of positive self-treatment? Why or why not?*

_____

_____

_____

7 Consider someone who loves you (mom, dad, spouse, etc.), how would they describe your positive identity? (Ex. Ralph is a kind-hearted...).

_____

_____

_____

_____

_____

_____

_____

8 How would <u>you</u> describe your authentic identity?

_____

_____

_____

_____

_____

_____

_____

_____

_____

_____

_____

_____

9 Do you believe that your addiction is in alignment with your authentic identity/self? Why or why not?

_____

_____

_____

_____

10 *How would your most authentic self view your addiction?*

_____

_____

_____

_____

11 *Choose all the adjectives that describe your authentic identity:*

☐ Powerful   ☐ Cares About Family

☐ Bold   ☐ Good Counsel

☐ Charismatic   ☐ Overcomes Obstacles

☐ Kind   ☐ Can Grow

☐ Generous   ☐ Attractive

☐ Loving   ☐ Resourceful

☐ Persistent   ☐ Insightful

☐ Strong   ☐ Adaptive

☐ Intelligent   ☐ Relational

☐ Capable   ☐ Other: _____

☐ Leads Others   ☐ Other: _____

12 *Do you believe you could use the positive qualities you mentioned above in your endeavor to end your addiction? Why or why not?*

_____

_____

_____

_____

13 *Describe your ideal life. Include components that your addiction may have prevented you from having hope for (owning a house, great relationship with spouse, etc.):*

_____

_____

_____

_____

_____

_____

_____

_____

_____

14 *When are you going to commit to your sobriety? The sooner the better.*

_____

_____

15 *Who are three people you are going to bring into your process? If you can't identify three, you may want to explore a support group to find understanding people.*

_____

_____

_____

Exercise:

On a sheet of paper, write 50 positive statements about yourself. Read through the list 7 days in a row. For example, "I am a powerful leader, I am a kind person, I am full of energy, I'm a naturally optimistic person." By engaging with your true nature, you'll begin retraining your mind to feel more positively about yourself...which will empower you to release any negative habits or patterns.

SUMMARY

In conclusion, becoming sober is a highly personal journey. It involves recognizing patterns that are destructive in our lives, and confronting them. It requires community and personal responsibility. It demands we mature in the way we view ourselves, and what is acceptable as self-treatment.

If you get disheartened, disillusioned, or disappointed; that's okay. It is part of the journey to have ups and downs. The most important thing is to make a firm decision. Your firm decision will make a thousand smaller decisions for you. For example, I'm going to stop drinking...so I can't go to bars anymore. If you don't have to make countless small decisions, you can use that energy to create life-giving activities and relationships to replace your addictive ones.

Ultimately, you will find that your addiction is a wet-blanket over your life. It shields you from the vibrancy, enjoyment, and intimacy of a fully-present life. The fleeting enjoyments you felt from your addiction will pale in comparison to the rich rewards from a fully-present lifestyle.

We, at How to Life Good, wish you the best on your journey and are confident you will do well! If you have struggles, feel free to connect with us on our facebook page or by visiting ***www.howtolifegood. com*** and sending us a note.

If you are in eminent harm, please call 911 or contact a medical professional immediately.

And as always, we're looking forward to your incredible testimonies.

All the Best!

Blair

 howtolifegood

Here is a calendar to get you started. You can "Check off" your days of sobriety so you can start to gain a foothold on a fully present life.

The day I will begin abstaining from my addiction is: _____

Sun	**Mon**	**Tue**	**Wed**	**Thu**	**Fri**	**Sat**

NOTES

NOTES

NOTES

NOTES

How to Shame Yourself, No.

Life Yourself, Love Yourself Good

Kicking Your Addictions in Their Stupid Face

How to "With"

Healthy and Pain-Free Bodies - Yes Please!

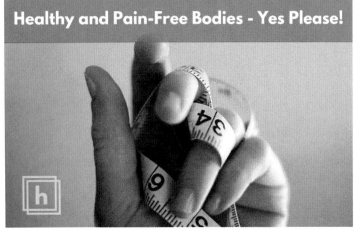

Breaking Family Rules that Suck

howtolifegood

SAVE 20%
ON YOUR NEXT PRODUCT AT HOWTOLIFEGOOD.COM
USING COUPON CODE *20percentoff*

Where Those Passions at Yo?

Healing Mom and Dad Crap

How to Romantic Relationship Good

Performance and Escape. Hard Pass

Finally Living the Fully You You

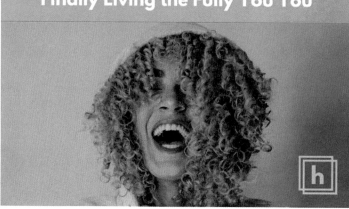

Well Hello Heart, Been Awhile

howtolifegood

Made in the USA
Columbia, SC
11 October 2020